Nail on the H
slaining

Paul Cookson is a poet and has been for most of his life. With over sixty titles to his name and well over a million sales, his poems have appeared in over two hundred anthologies. He is Poet in Residence at The National Football Museum and Everton in the Community, and the band Slade have proclaimed him their Poet Laureate. With Martin Chatterton, Paul recently launched *Bluenoses*, a weekly children's show on YouTube with animated features, a poem and an illustration. More details can be found at worldofbluenoses.com. Paul has also released an album with Don Powell's Occasional Flames, *Just My Cup of Tea* (co-written and performed with Les Glover and Don Powell from Slade). *Classic Rock* and *Vive Le Rock* both scored it 8/10. As well as writing poems throughout lockdown, Paul also grew a beard of varying shades. For more information visit paulcooksonpoet.co.uk and follow his poems via Twitter, Facebook and Instagram.

Chris Riddell OBE is a South African-born English illustrator, children's author and political cartoonist for the *Observer*. He has won three Kate Greenaway Medals (the librarians' award for the best illustrated children's book), and books that he has either illustrated or written have won the Nestlé Smarties Book Prize three times. Chris has illustrated numerous works, from J.M. Barrie and Lewis Carroll to J.K. Rowling and Michael Rosen, and has frequently collaborated with Paul Stewart, Brian Patten and Neil Gaiman – to name just a few. He was appointed the UK Children's Laureate in 2015.

Korky Paul was born in Harare, Zimbabwe in 1951 and enjoyed a wild and privileged childhood in the African bush veldt. He studied Fine Arts at Durban Art School in South Africa and Film Animation at CalArts in California, and began his career in advertising before becoming an award-winning illustrator of children's books. Among his many picture books are the multi-million selling *Winnie and Wilbur* series, the *Sir Scallywag* capers with Giles Andreae, and poetry anthologies featuring Paul Cookson. Korky is a patron of Pegasus Theatre, ARCh, Reading Quest and The Stratford Literary Festival, and winner of Supporter of the Year for Summertown Stars AFC. He works and lives in Oxford and Greece.

Martin Chatterton was born in Liverpool and divides his working year between the UK and Australia. A full-time writer, illustrator, film-maker and performer, he has illustrated more than a hundred books, including for Roger McGough, Tony Bradman, Julia Donaldson, Jon Blake, Tony Mitton and Michael Rosen. Martin has written many children's books for a variety of age ranges, and also writes crime fiction and for the screen as Ed Chatterton. He is a founding partner in Hungry Head Productions (UK), and his recent work includes Penguin children's book *The Tell*, many of the *Middle School series* (with James Patterson), as well as writing and illustrating the award-winning picture book, *Winter of the White Bear* – which is now in production as an animated feature. Martin and Paul's latest collaboration is *Bluenoses*, a weekly animated YouTube channel for children.

NAIL ON THE HEAD
PAUL COOKSON

A COVID-19 POETRY DIARY
VOLUME 4

Illustrated by Chris Riddell,
Korky Paul & Martin Chatterton

Flapjack Press
flapjackpress.co.uk

Exploring the synergy between performance and the page

Published in 2021 by Flapjack Press
Salford, Gtr Manchester
⊕ flapjackpress.co.uk
f Flapjack Press ✖ FlapjackPress ▶ Flapjack Press

ISBN 978-1-8381185-2-5

Illustrations copyright © Chris Riddell OBE, 2021
Pages 1, 18, 21, 22, 31, 34, 37, 41, 43, 48 & 51
⊕ chrisriddellblog.tumblr.com ✖ chrisriddell50 ⊚ chris_riddell

Illustrations copyright © Korky Paul, 2021
Pages 1, 57, 63, 71, 73, 79, 82, 86, 89, 93 & 96
⊕ korkypaul.com ✖ korkypaul ⊚ korkypaul

Illustrations copyright © Martin Chatterton, 2021
Pages 1, 11, 12, 99, 106, 109, 110, 113, 116, 122, 124, 129, 135 & 138
Cover by Martin Chatterton
⊕ worldofchatterton.com ✖ MEChatterton ⊚ edchatt

Printed by Imprint Digital, Exeter, Devon
⊕ digital.imprint.co.uk

FSC

A UNESCO City
of Literature

† Published by Flapjack Press
• Published by A Twist in the Tale & available at paulcooksonpoet.co.uk
★ Published by Pan Macmillan ♦ Published by Otter Barry Books
▲ Published by Bloomsbury

Contents

What can I say that I haven't said in the introductions for the first three collections?

Four books and over five hundred poems. Lockdown to so-called "Freedom Day". You never plan this far ahead, but it doesn't just happen either.

Special thanks to Paul at Flapjack Press for his faith and support in this project. The easiest and quickest four books I have ever been involved with. Particular mention to fellow poet Henry Normal who pointed me towards Paul and Flapjack. It's your fault Henry.

Equally, Martin Chatterton for the iconic covers and illustrations. Talking of which – Chris Riddell and Korky Paul … an honour and a pleasure to be on the same page as the three of you. So pleased we shared this book together. Felt about right.

I've done several shows based on these collections and re-reading, re-visiting and picking out the poems to perform it's great to see how many stand the test of time in their own right and not just as a diary entry of "that day".

I'm not sure where go next regarding books – but rest assured I will write a poem a day for as long as I can. I want to be the man of a thousand poems.

Oh … and I'm now available for performances in schools, arts centres, libraries and assorted front rooms as I have a few books to sell.

Huge and heartfelt thanks to all.

Paul Cookson
October 2021

Nail on the Head

Cut From the Same Cloth These Days

#393 / 23:03:2021

I have lost trust in politicians
All of them, pretty much

However, reading that phrase
Implies I trusted some of them
Sometime

As a young man they all seemed to be
Older men who seemed to have "done something"
... as in had a real job
Before going into politics
So at least had some experience of real life

Even if you didn't agree with them
At least they had some sort of gravitas

Now
Most of them look the same
All too young
No experience of working life to guide them

Not about sides either
Just happens to be "them" at the moment
So we can't really judge the others
Apart from the fact
They seem ineffectual so far
Maybe they are just waiting

But this lot
The grey mafia of incompetence
The amorphous blob of ... nothingness

Two years ago
They must have thought they'd got it made
Landslide victory
Massive majority
Five years of easy pootling along

And then Covid
Bang
Lockdown
Boom

And here they are
Dithering
Wavering in the wind
Clueless and corrupt
Not a decision of note between them
All promoted beyond their means

So yes, I have lost faith in politicians
I've sworn at the telly daily
For a long, long time now
And I'm sick of it
Totally

Mortal Yet Immortal

#394 / 24:03:2021
For Peter Lorimer and Frank Worthington

Neither played for our teams of choice
But playing football every school playtime
Or on the rec every Saturday afternoon
We always wanted to be like you

Your names – not just football legends
Immortal to those of us of an uncertain age
But names that became verbs
Part of our everyday games

A power-blaster past the keeper
And we'd done a "Lorimer"
Keepy-uppies, a juggle, a twist, turn and shot
"Oh what a Worthington!"

Men defined by the perfect moments
They created, week in, week out
We defined ourselves by trying
To recreate those self-same moments

And those magical moments
Remind us of a different time
Not just when we were young
But when footballers were ordinary gods

Heroes? Yes
Superstars? Yes
Legends? Yes
But everyday ordinary blokes who were gods

Soon there will come a time
When we say
"They don't make them like they used to
Last of a dying breed ..."

Peter Lorimer and Frank Worthington
Mortal yet immortal
We thank you and salute you
And we will never forget

I'm Not Wasting More Than Two Lines on This Phrase That Shows His True Colours and Tells Us Everything We Need to Know

#395 / 25:03:2021

Not a chance he's misunderstood
When he says "greed is good"

Anniversary Poem

#396 / 26:03:2021

(I wrote my first poem of this series a year ago – after the first doorstep applause for the N.H.S. – and when the project became a book, I went back and retrospectively wrote the first three poems to fit in with the concept.)

A year ago today
I wrote a poem called 'Connection'
That may seem a strange admission from a poet
Writing a poem – but it isn't

There were days, weeks even
And I wouldn't write a new poem
I'd perform poems every day, all round the country
And – in doing so
Not have the time to write

Then that stopped. Overnight.
Work disappeared. Changed.
Time suddenly on my hands
As the world tilted on its axis

So, with nothing else to do
I wrote a poem
Then another
And another

I didn't know then
That it would become a daily occurrence
But it did
And it has

Neither did I know then
That it would turn into three books

Yes, three new books in one year
And nearly four hundred new poems

You have been my audience
Virtual applause on a daily basis
You have also been my inspiration
My encouragement and my purpose

Who knows what the future holds
But here we all are
Still writing
Still lots to write about

And long may we continue
In this daily communion
Whatever form it takes
Peace be with you

Shopping Malady

#397 / 27:03:2021

In the shopping centre
Four young men strut lazily
Flouting not only the one-way system
But also the request for face coverings

They are loud
And unaware of everyone else
Nobody says anything
No security asks them to cover up

So they do just what they want
As they want, regardless
I am glad of my own mask
They cannot hear the words I call them

Or if they do
They can't prove it

The Words of Mother Abagail

#398 / 28:03:2021

(Mother Abagail is a character in my favourite book, Stephen King's The Stand.*)*

The words of Mother Abagail
Ringing like a bell
God has got great things for you to do
You say you don't believe in him
Well, that don't matter much
Why? ... He believes in you

Prophecy or heresy
Foolishness or lie
Or messages from heaven that are true?
Either way, you've got to make your choice
And take a stand
Why? ... He believes in you

Weasels in the cornfield
Rats are in the barn
Shadows that surround the chosen few
Oh ye of little faith
You will find the strength
Why? ... He believes in you

The words of Mother Abagail
Like a silent psalm
A prayer to hold as we're all passing through
The valley of the shadows
On to the other side
Why? ... He believes in you

Faith or hope or doubt
Truth or disbelief

God has still got things we all must do
In the words of Mother Abagail
All these things shall pass
Why? … He believes in you

Read the sordid stories if you must
Is this someone that we all can trust?

We Live in Hope

#400 / 30·03·2021

The sun shone brighter
Blue sky warmth and tee-shirt sleeves
My usual walk

Past the school at playtime
Invigorated by voices of happy children
Shouting, playing, laughing

And in that moment
It could be any time at all
Any year, not this one

Life being lived
Time being enjoyed
Long may it continue

If Boris Johnson Was Harry Carpenter

#401 / 31:03:2021
(A cinquain – 5 lines, 2, 4, 6, 8, 2 syllables.)

Jab jab
A quick one two
We've got it on the ropes
Winning the fight against Covid
Jab jab

Summery ... Or Summary?

#402 / 01:04:2021

The first day for shorts
And a longer walk
That takes me across the fields
And to the canal

Sun on my face
Birdsong in my ears
Not a human in sight
Alone apart from one brown duck

If I close my eyes and relax
I could be anywhere
Untroubled and carefree
Until I put my hand in my pocket

The mask is there ... waiting
A reminder that the bad times
Are not behind us
And normality a way off yet

One Consequence is of the Consequences

#403 / 02:04:2021

There is talk and fear
A third wave on the horizon
In these times of strangeness
Nothing's now surprising

Adapt, survive, continue
Carry on come what may
And even worse – you're cursed with verse
I'll have the time for a poem a day

Measuring Life in Multiples of Seventeen

#404 / 03:04:2021

I've started wearing
My watch again in the hope
That times are changing

And started to think
In seventeen syllables
A human haiku

Sun Rise Service

#405 / 04:04:2021

Easter Sunday in the seventies
Always started in the darkness

Members of our church would congregate
On the gentle slopes of Beacon Fell

As dawn broke we would sing hymns
Listen anew to resurrection stories

Then go back to the church hall
For bacon, eggs, beans and hot tea

The cold of the morning air
Watching darkness become light

Always brought things to life again
Seeing the sun actually rise

Sun rise
More than just play on words

Progress?

#406 / 05:04:2021

Now numbers are not at their peak
The future is looking less bleak
This road map to freedom
Shows how we're proceedin'
With two tests now every week

Countdown to Normal

#407 / 06:04:2021

Countdown to normal
We cannot wait for everyday routines
Desperate for the regular

Haircuts, shops and workouts
The communion of sport and art
Beer and restaurant tables

The little things we've missed
Bigger with each passing day
Absence makes the heart grow

So long we have been distant
Necessarily anti-social
Craving connection and contact

Countdown to normal
Proceed with caution
Not there yet

Some Days

#408 / 07:04:2021

Some days
I don't feel like writing poems
But I said I would
So here I am again
A man of my word
Sat at the dining room table
Notebook open
The fourth so far
(Notebooks that is, not tables)
And pen in hand
Looking for inspiration
Waiting for the magic
When mostly it isn't magic
But just following the trail of the words
As one leads to another
Then another
And another
Until we have this …
A poem
Of sorts
That doesn't rhyme

If I Was You Mr Williamson
I Would Choose My Words Very Carefully
(As Indeed I Have When Writing This Two-Verse Haiku)

#409 / 08:04:2021

Oh the irony
Discipline and order show
Your double standards

How can a man in
Charge of education still
Remain ignorant?

Eternal Optimist

#410 / 09:04:2021

Two days of sunshine
Out came the shorts
Off came the beard

One week later
These actions seem premature
And somewhat foolish

I thought my hat and gloves
Had been banished
Until the autumn

Apparently not
Walking in the wind and snow
My chin is suddenly colder

Grief and Loss are Grief and Loss

#411 / 10:04:2021

Someone's granddad died today
Someone's father passed away

Someone's husband – laid to rest
Someone loved – someone blessed

Private view, public glare
Ever present – always there

All the things we never saw
Behind the scenes, behind the door

Just like every family
Every day – a memory

A glance, a touch, a quip, a joke
Things he did and words he spoke

Human, flawed – the man he was
But grief and loss are grief and loss

Those who love are those who grieve
Those who mourn for those who leave

Those who leave who leave their mark
Are carried in each heavy heart

Love is love – come what may
Someone cherished – died today

Unguarded

#412 / 11:04:2021

In the midst of pomp and ceremony
A joke

In the midst of protocol and circumstance
A well-planned prank

A moment of surprise
A snapshot of lightness and humanity

You – the guard
Caught her – off guard

And her smile said everything
The Queen and her joker

A truly royal flush

Fling Wide the Doors

#413 / 12:04:2021

Open the gyms, the bars and the stores
Unlock the shops, fling wide the doors
Welcome back beers – sound the applause
Hooray for haircuts – fling wide the doors

A little normality – back on these shores
Head to the high street – fling wide the doors
Responsibility – take time to pause
Think about others – fling wide the doors

Don't be the reason – don't be the cause
For flinging wide open – hospital doors

The Business of Buzzing Crowds
#414 / 13:04:2021

Like ants on an ice cream that's spilt on the floor
The madness of masses that gather galore
The swarming's a warning we should not ignore

Making the most of this new situation
Social and sunshine – a welcome elation
An over-reaction to long isolation …

Retail relief – the high streets are seething
It beggars belief – beer gardens heaving
Just what is the truth that we are believing?

The road map to freedom is already tattered
As personal freedom is all that has mattered
Let's hope that the virus hasn't been scattered …

Sign of the Times
#415 / 14:04:2021

Gents so unkempt, they loiter in streets
Embarrassed – they gaze at their shoes
Waiting and watching – long-haired in the heat
It's the time for – barber queues

#416 / 15:04:2021

It's true – we don't know all of the facts
It's true – we don't understand
What's also true – because it is you
It's probably underhand

One rule for the plebs and the peasants
A different one for the toffs
Stereotypes and mixed metaphors
Fat cat mates – snouts in troughs

#417 / 16:04:2021

Cash for questions, cronyism – corruption guaranteed
Money talks and silences those who deal in greed
Truth has been a casualty … nobody grieves
Why? Because you're all as
Thick as thieves

Transparency now clouded – lines are grey and blurred
Your mouths may be moving but we don't believe a word
Unopposed – ranks are closed – you do just as you please
Why? Because you're all as
Thick as thieves

Trust has been eroded – principles – well, none
Accountable for actions – disappeared and gone
You've got a code of conduct that nobody believes
Why? Because you're all as
Thick as thieves

We know that hands are dirty and pockets have been lined
No interest in an inquest – the only thing you'll find
Evidence of negligence? Nothing up your sleeves
Why? Because you're all as
Thick as thieves

No beginning and no end to all the Tory sleaze
Why? Because you're all as thick as thieves
There's no vaccination – no end to this disease
We must all be thick
And you are thieves

A Family

#418 / 17:04:2021

A family gathers to say goodbye
Private grief, public eye

A family gathers to pay respect
Recall, remember and reflect

A family gathers to say farewell
A life well-lived, a life lived well

A day for closure and release
Let a family grieve in peace

His Favourite Cap

#419 / 18:04:2021

His favourite cap
Always wore it

Never without it
Unless indoors

Loved it more
Than other hats he had to wear

More him, just him
At home, comfortable

His favourite cap
Fitting

Supermarket Flowers

#420 / 19:04:2021

For the second weekend running
I made the two-hundred-mile round trip
For a garden cup of tea with mum
Stopping only to buy supermarket cakes
And a bunch of flowers

She rang in the week
To tell me how beautiful they still are
And haven't they lasted well
No doubt she'll ring this week
And say the same about the cheap tulips

It's the little things
I suppose
We are making up for lost time
And time we may not always have

That
And still being able
To buy flowers
For the living

Spectacular Own Goal

#421 / 20:04:2021

It's all about the money
But this – a brand new low
European Super League
Not the way to go

By the few and for the few
It's remote control
The day that football sold its soul
Spectacular own goal

Out of touch and out of reach
Disregard for fans
Forget about the football
It's just financial plans

Digging down for further gold
Deepening the hole
The day that football sold its soul
Spectacular own goal

Tearing up remaining roots
Severing tradition
Ignoring all the history
That gave them this position

Blinkered and self-serving
No respect at all
The day that football sold its soul
Spectacular own goal

Not even based on merit
Just the chosen few
Blatant profiteering
Though that is nothing new

Complete and utter disregard
Just climb that greasy pole
The day that football sold its soul
Spectacular own goal

The grass that seems much greener
Means you will walk alone
As football is divided by
The green greed grass of home

All fans now united
Revolted on the whole
The day that football sold its soul
Spectacular own goal

Just Because

#422 / 21:04:2021

Just because what happened yesterday
Doesn't mean that the problem's gone away
Greed and football – here and here to stay

Just because the six have all retreated
Doesn't mean that greed has been defeated
Or that these mistakes will not be repeated

Just because the numbers now are thinning
Doesn't mean that people power is winning
Remember this – they signed up – when it was beginning

Just because it's now about to fail
Doesn't mean that it wasn't a betrayal
When everything it seems is always up for sale

Just because they tweet the tweets, making the right sound
Doesn't mean that they are standing on their moral ground
Common sense and honesty have only just been found

Just because you're backing out of this situation
Doesn't mean you're saving your tarnished reputation
Or that you should be exempt from recrimination

When somebody can earn a fee in just one day
The wages of a nurse who is on full pay
There'll never be a thing that we can call fair play

Just because – what happened yesterday
Doesn't mean that greed is going to go away
The game that once was beautiful – now, only just okay

A Step in the Right Direction

#423 / 21:04:2021

Yesterday was different
For the first time in months
I had to think about shoes
Actual shoes
Not slippers or trainers

Also, a button-up shirt
Not a tee shirt with a band name on

And a shave
Not beardy stubble
(Which could be a band name)

Yes, I was up early
And driving to Hull
To a favourite school

Back to work
For a day anyway

Today, back at home
Writing poems

And looking at the diary
No longer totally blank

Short and Sweet

#424 / 22:04:2021

I've got a daily poem to write
Before I do my weekly shop
Just got time – four lines that rhyme
Then I'd better stop

For England, Shakespeare and Saint George

#425 / 23:04:2021

Rule Britannia
Raise your glasses
For England, Shakespeare and Saint George

Fly the flag
Be proud of our heritage
For England, Shakespeare and Saint George

Gather solemnly, not in churches
But pub gardens
For England, Shakespeare and Saint George

Is this a lager I see before me?
To beer or not to beer?
That is the question

Charge your glasses
Toast our great country
And sing our anthem loud and proud

'ere we go – 'ere we go – 'ere we go

A Birthday is Never a Birthday When So Close to a Funeral
#426 / 24:04:2021

Apparently
I missed your birthday

What with everything else going on
It slipped under my radar

Not that I've ever sent you a card
And even if I did

There's no certainty it would reach you
Or that you would read it

But it must have been a strange one
Your first alone after all this time

So even if I'd sent a card
It wouldn't have included the word "Happy"

I can only hope that it passed unremarkably
Ma'am

It's Coming to Something When ...

#427 / 25:04:2021

The man who can't be trusted
On a man who can't be trusted
Has come back done and dusted
For the man who had him busted

Get Some Sense of Perspective ...
Or Just Get Some Sense

#428 / 26:04:2021

India – tens of thousands die
As Covid keeps on breeding

London – thousands march and shout
About their personal freedom

Let the Bodies Pile Up High

#429 / 27:04:2021

Let nature take its natural course
Let's live and then let die
I'm Bond and Covid's Blofeld
Let the bodies pile up high

Let's stand and face the danger
Squarely in the eye
Face to face and standing firm
Let the bodies pile up high

Let's not get round to lockdown
Heed my battle cry
And carry on regardless
Let the bodies pile up high

The stench of death upon my hands
May well intensify
But let's not get distracted
Let the bodies pile up high

You know me all too well by now
Could you believe that I
Could utter something heartless
Let the bodies pile up high

Oh Dominic, my Judas
Would have you crucify
For words I never ever said
Let the bodies pile up high

Let's get this in proportion
And let's not magnify
Or take it out of context
Let the bodies pile up high

The truth! The truth! What is the truth?
I'll honestly deny
The words that ever left my mouth
Let the bodies pile up high

The truth, the truth and nothing but
A barefaced shameless lie
Watch my lips – they didn't say
Let the bodies pile up high

Let the bodies pile up
Stack them up a mile up
Let the bodies pile up in their thousands way up high
Let the failures pile up
Before I tear the file up
Of everything I should have done but let it all slip by

"LET THE BODIES PILE UP HIGH"

Words Fail

#130 / 28:04:2021

I'll be honest
This is not so much of a poem
As a response

An angry response
Blood boiling and …
Just angry

Words fail

To take to the streets
In the midst of a pandemic
Is one thing

But to appropriate
The Star of David
And make Holocaust comparisons …

Words fail

This is not about "personal liberty"
Or "freedom of speech"
Or "the right to protest"

You are free to believe
To believe whatever you want
As am I, as are we all

You are also free to speak about it
However crackpot or conspiracy-based
But …

But

To compare yourselves with the Holocaust
Words fail
Words just fail

To have so little comprehension
So little respect for others
Zero perspective in the pursuit of your own agenda

That you stoop
Stoop
Yes, stoop so low

Words fail

Curtains for Mr Johnson

#431 / 29:04:2021

Firstly
Don't trust anyone
Who doesn't like John Lewis

Secondly
Don't trust anyone
Who doesn't know what true is

The Wheels on the Bus

#432 / 30·04·2021

The wheels on the bus are falling off
Falling off – falling off
The wheels on the bus are falling off
Day by day

The deals of the boss are turning up
Turning up – turning up
The deals of the boss are turning up
Day by day

The sleaze and the fuss is building now
Building now – building now
The sleaze and the fuss is building now
Day by day

Haiku of Truth

#433 / 30:04:2021

"Nothing to see here"
That's correct – you seem to be
Hiding everything

All This Talk of Decoration While Half a World Away ...

#434 / 01:05:2021

Raging fires
Funeral pyres
Horrors still unfold
Thousands lost
Uncounted cost
Oxygen is gold

Haik-U.S.A.

#435 / 02:05:2021

I've not written much
About you recently so
Things must be better

The bar set so low
They couldn't be much worse so
Not a lot to beat

Live from Manchester

#436 / 03:05:2021

Some people are on the pitch
The players aren't

Lost the Plocht ... Definitely

#437 / 04:05:2021

Whacht?
A royal yacht?
Two hundred million
In these times?
Surely nocht

In Other News

#438 / 05:05:2021

It was reassuring to know
That after all this time
I didn't fluff my lines
Remembered my carefully rehearsed ad libs
Timed the old poems and jokes to perfection
And even thought of two new puns

Back in school
Back in front of an audience
Doing what I do best
And loving it

X Marks the Spot

#439 / 06:05:2021

Piracy – alive and well
Money in that pot
Ill-gotten gains and raids
X marks the spot

There was a map for freedom
Seems they've lost the plot
No sense of direction
X marks the spot

Time to stand against the crimes
Time to stop the rot
Every voice is vital
X marks the spot

The pencil – mightier than the sword
On a string is all we've got
The ballot box, no treasure chest
X marks the spot

One Good Turn

#440 / 07:05:2021

Out of the blue
A man I knew
But didn't really, really know
Sent me a message on a Friday afternoon

Unexpectedly generous
This act of kindness and belief
Was affirmation and trust
He saw the potential and thought of me

A heart bigger than Manchester
One good turn
And indeed he is
Yes, one good turn preserves another

Dear Mister Starmer

#441 / 08:05:2021

You seem to have a problem.
No-one knows who you really are
Or what it is you stand for

Your suit is nicer than the last one's
And your hair is neater than his
But we're not even sure how to pronounce your name

Keith …
You seem like a nice enough chap
And sound intelligent on the telly

Especially on *Prime Minister's Questions*
When you speak in sentences
But we still don't know who you really are

Or what you stand for
And that's the problem
It's all a bit … well, grey

You're all a bit grey
Labour used to be red, bright red
Working man stuff, power to the people stuff

But now you're just … grey
And if you can't beat this shower
Then there's no hope for you

Or us either, for that matter
So Kevin – or whatever your name is
Get your act together

Otherwise we're stuck with this lot of clowns
I mean, I don't like 'em at all
But at least I know what we're getting

Or not getting
And I can trust their untrustworthiness
But you and your lot …

Who knows?
Certainly not you eh, Keith
Just be better than them – that's all we ask

Better the Devil You Know

#442 / 09:05:2021

Aye, I know he's a bit of a devil
But at least you know
Where you stand with him, like

Yes, he tells lies
But don't they all, them lot?
It's what they do these days

At least he smiles and he's jolly
Not like the others
A bit po-faced and boring if you ask me

He's a bit of a laugh though
A bit of a lad
Wish he'd brush his hair, mind

To be honest
Don't know what the others stand for
Bit grey if truth be told

At least this new one's
Not the old one
Him? I would not trust

At all
Like I said
Better the devil you know eh?

There is Promise in Compromise

#443 / 10:05:2021

There is a fight to be had
A battle to be won
But not with each other

First and foremost
Get rid of the real enemy
That is the job in hand

Put aside your party prejudice
Lay down your preconceptions
Accept the broad way forward

Everything else can be worked out
But first things first
Compromise is not a dirty word

Compromise is listening to all
Respecting differences
Uniting for the common good

Better to compromise with each
And win than to splinter
Disintegrate and lose again

Compromise is not a sign of weakness
But a show of strength
A position of grace

There is no moral high ground
Even though some would like to claim it
Stand on it and shout down

Compromise has promise
And that is the start
But with any compromise
The promise must be kept

What Have They Really Done for Us?

#444 / 11:05:2021

Nine new food banks in our town
N-I-N-E ... that spells nine
Labour gave us nowt like that
So the Tories get my vote this time

So ... All's Well That Ends Well ...

#445 / 12:05:2021

Hope in our hearts – the end is in sight
Once in the tunnel – we now see the light
Remember the facts
That paper the cracks
As Boris will claim that he got it all right

Something I've Been Meaning to Do

#446 / 13.05.2021

I've been meaning to write a poem
About mental health
All week

But I've had a lot on my mind
Plus there's always something else in the news
Always something else to talk about

I mean, there's lots going on
That you don't know about
But you know how it is

There's always something
That seems more important
Something to distract

Always the case
And then, when I do, like now
It's this, it's rushed

And it barely scratches the surface
We really must talk more
Sometime

The Government That's Murdering the Arts

#447 / 14:05:2021

The butchers have arrived
The abattoir's alive
This is where and how it all just starts
A rusty blade that slices
Where our cultural life is
The government that's murdering the arts

No disguising and no hiding
The slope on which we're sliding
The horses – overtaken by the carts
Values are diminished
If expression is now finished
The government that's murdering the arts

Importance is reflected
In the funding that's collected
And the funding sum is less than all the parts
The proof is in your pounds and pence
Instead of just plain common sense
The government that's murdering the arts

Difficult to put back
All of that you cut back
So don't cut back at all and leave your marks
We know your hearts aren't in it
If you're prepared to bin it
The government that's murdering the arts

This sickening decision
Of ignorant precision
A dagger blow that's straight into our hearts

The importance of the earnest
Whose purse strings are the firmest
The government that's murdering the arts

Maverick invention
Expression and intention
Must be allowed the freedom to catch sparks
Not stilting the creation
Of a future generation
The government that's murdering the arts

Almost Forgotten

#448 / 15:05:2021

It doesn't feel like it
But it is today
FA Cup Final Day

A day that was looked forward to
Special – last game of the season
The gleaming jewel on football's crown
A day when the world would stop
And dads would get their jobs done before kick off
Always three o'clock
Watching every bit of the build up
Team themed *It's a Knockout*
Team themed *A Question of Sport*
Getting excited by the sight
Of a bus on a dual carriageway stuck in traffic
Then parking at Wembley
Players in the Sunday best suits
Like a wedding stag party
Testing the pitch in shiny shoes
Seeing "The road to Wembley"
Again and again, goals on muddy pitches
All to the backing of a hastily recorded dodgy song
Picking a team to support for the day
Even though it wasn't yours
And if it was against a team you hated – even better
Yes, FA Cup Final Day was special
Not so much now
Just another match on the telly

I'll still be watching though
C'mon Leicester!
What time's kick off?

It's the Sound of the Crowd That Punctuates the Game

#449 / 16:05:2021

The sound of the crowd
A well-timed tackle that brings the cheers
A shot well wide that brings the jeers

The sound of the crowd
A wonder goal ignites the roars
Delirium and wild applause

The sound of the crowd
World class saves – the *oohs* and *aaahs*
The sweet relief of VAR

The sound of the crowd
Unlocked jubilation flows
As that final whistle blows

The sound of the crowd
All that pent-up shared emotion
Players' efforts, team devotion

The sound of the crowd
Players, owner – raise that cup
A city united – lifted up

A Good Reason for a Hug and a Haiku

#450 / 17:05:2021

Today's the day I
Start my first full week of work
In over a year

There Will Be Hugs

#451 / 18:05:2021

Even though free to hug at last
I did not do so

But then again, I wasn't
Meeting old friends on a workday Monday

Random hugging of strangers
Did not seem appropriate, however legal

But I did shake hands for the first time
In a long, long time and that felt good

Those of you I know and love
And haven't seen, get ready ...

There will be hugs

I'd Forgotten How Much I Love My Job

#452 / 19:05:2021

Time fades memories
The normal changes
As new routines fall uneasily into place

Not driving the length and breadth of the country
No schools and laughter, no shows
Some things I didn't miss, some I did

And now, one week back on track
A week like "the old days"
And I'd forgotten how much I love my job

The laughter, the jokes, more laughter
But it's always about the poetry
The magic of words

A few lines from yesterday's poems
Words and ideas – not mine
But the children's …

Super-Teacher – Zoom
Flies around the room
Purple pants of course – Nursery

Summer, autumn, winter, spring
A little bit of everything
Year one – four seasons in one poem

Don't plant your pants dad
To "sisters together, sister forever" and Emmeline Pankhurst
Year two – all within forty minutes

Things to do with SATS – feed them to the fish
Flush 'em down the loo to year six memories
All in the same hour

Things we take away from here
Ibrahim in the cupboard
Scared of the snake in nursery

Every school nativity – I was always the donkey
Every school nativity – she was always the cow
The best friends we ever made

Yes, the laughter, the emotion, the connection
The magic of poetry
I'd forgotten how much I love my job

Yet

#453 / 20:05:2021

I went to the pub
For the first time in
... well, who knows

Beer, steak, football
That was the plan
I was alone, after all

Firstly, they wouldn't put my match on
Steak – good but not spectacular
Chips – passable

I thought the beer would taste better
It didn't
Was just okay

Wasn't as excited as I thought I'd be
Underwhelmed at best
Not just because I was alone

It's everyone else
Some seemed too loud, too casual
As if none of this had ever happened

I like the fact that things are opening
That I'm starting to work again
But ...

Part of me likes the caution
The consideration of others
Maybe I'm not ready for lots of other people

Yet

Great to See You John, Really Great

#454 / 21:05:2021

I don't think we'd ever hugged before
Ever
But after nearly forty years
Outside a coffee shop in the rain

We did

Not just because we could
But because it was good ...
Good to see you my friend
After all this time ... in these times

A great big bear hug of an embrace
And the years just slipped
We laughed, caught up
And laughed some more

Two old men talking about youth
And being an age we'd never considered
But two old friends talking about the present
And the future too

Music and connection
Songs unwritten, things still left to do
Until it was time to brave the rain once more
Another bear hug – twice in one day

A forty-year-old embrace
One thing is for sure
At our age
It won't be forty years before the next one

The Teachers Don't Talk in the Staffroom

#455 / 22:05:2021

The teachers don't talk in the staffroom
When they are all on their break
Voices are mumbling
Tummies are rumbling
Looking forward to ... cake!

The teachers don't talk in the staffroom
Are they asleep or awake?
We found out why
When peeping inside ...
Their mouths are full of ... cake!

The teachers don't talk in the staffroom
But oh! The noises they make
Are chomping and chewing
What are they doing?
Stuffing their faces with ... cake!

The teachers don't talk in the staffroom
So much time that they take ...
On slices too big
They eat like a ...
Gobbling lots of ... cake!

The teachers don't talk in the staffroom
They all have tummy ache
Grunting and groaning
All of them moaning ...
I've eaten too much ... cake!

The teachers don't talk in the staffroom
But they are all putting on weight
Forgetting their diet
It's just like a riot
Racing to get to the … cake!
Chasing to get to the … cake!
Fighting to get the best … cake!

Apology Poem

#456 / 22:05:2021

Now I'm feeling guilty
That today's poem
Although new to you was indeed
"One I prepared earlier"

So I'm writing this
Something new
Obviously it won't be as good
As the one I shared

But it will be new
Professional pride I suppose
Like *Mastermind*
"I've started so I'll finish"

Although, to be honest
I'm not sure
If there'll ever be a finish
To all this

Or the poetry

A Small Truth
#457 / 23:05:2021

Driving to my mother's
I see a sign with an arrow
Asmall CP school

Of course I read it as
A small CP school
And imagine model village scenario

But I know for a fact
That any school, however small
Always has a massive heart

What Trickery is This Regarding the British Weather?
#458 / 24:05:2021

What trickery is this?
Is there something that I've missed?
Something I've forgotten to remember?

The sun shone yesterday
I went to bed in May
And seem to have awoken in November

The Times, They Changed Because of You

#459 / 25:05:2021
(Bob Dylan was 80 yesterday)

One man, six strings and poetry
That chimed so clear and rang so true
Right place, right face, right voice and choice
The times they changed because of you

A genius and a joker man
Unpredictable but always new
The magic and mystique, original, unique
The times they changed because of you

Legacy in turns of phrase
A spokesman for the few
A ragged rambling rolling truth
The times they changed because of you

We can't resist the words that twist
Each simple phrase that grew and grew
Now universal language used
The times they changed because of you

Questions, riddles, answers,
All tangled up in red and blue
Foolishness and wisdom mix
The times they changed because of you

Sometime god-like reputation
A Jesus and a Judas too
Acoustic then electric, authentic then heretic
The times they changed because of you

A hurricane of chaos
A brand new wind that's blowing through
Heaven's door ajar
The times they changed because of you

The Man We Didn't Trust Prepares to Tell Us About The Man We Still Don't Trust

#460 / 26:05:2021

So the man behind the man
Reveals there was no plan
As we suspected all along
When all of this began

Defences at the ready
"Well, we got the big things right
Anyone can be
Professors of hindsight"

Big things – like mortality
All who didn't survive
If you'd done the little things so well
More would be alive

Eleven Nights in Eccles ... And I Got No Eccles Cake

#461 / 27:05:2021

I'm back on the road again
After all this time
Eating on my own again
At the age of fifty-nine
Found coffee houses, burger bars
But here is my mistake
Eleven nights in Eccles
And no sign of a cake

When I'm here in Lancashire
My pot is always hot
And just like George I've got a little
Stick of Blackpool rock
And then I dream of Aberdeen
And a juicy Angus steak
But eleven nights in Eccles
And still no sign of cake

I've had a bun from Chelsea
I've had my Eton Mess
Worcester Sauce on my Scotch Egg
Melton Mowbray pork pies – yes!
A Bakewell tart to soothe my heart
But still I yearn and ache
Eleven nights in Eccles
And still no sign of cake

Give me a Cornish pasty
With a side of Cheddar cheese
A Yorkshire pudding stood in
A plate of Scouse but please
Just one bite of this delight
My tastebuds will awake
But eleven nights in Eccles
And still no sign of cake

No moist and spicy currants
No sugared buttered bake
I got no flaky pastry
I got no Eccles cake

Shock! Horror! Some of Us Have Always Felt That

#462 / 28:05:2021

Once united in cahoots
The main manipulator
Now – divided chaos
The teacher has turned traitor

Once the puller of the strings
Once the chief advisor
The gloves are off, the strings are cut
Are we any wiser?

Solidarity of conspirators
No longer ever-present
It's every man for himself
As things become unpleasant

If that's the way it is with them
Then how much more with us?
Over eighties and the weak ...
Throw them underneath the bus

The bus of hollow promises
But full of death and lies
No loyalty, no morals
And sadly no surprise

So, Mister Hancock …
#463 / 29.05.2021

"A minor breach of the rules"
The conclusion that they reach

They concentrate on "minor"
When it really should be "breach"

Respect
#464 / 30:05:2021

Second vaccination – yes
Thanks, God bless the N.H.S.

Safer maybe – peace of mind
Relief – well, of a kind

Less risk of infection
One small step in the right direction

The longer danger hasn't passed
Still I choose to wear my mask

A royal yacht
Why not?
Just what we all need

Make it a priority
For that small minority
Just what we all need

The N.H.S. is sinking
So just what are they thinking?
Just what we all need

Rather have a boat
Than keep the hospitals afloat
Just what we all need

All those bodies overboard
Are they bothered, overawed?
Just what we all need

Already been titanic
But still no need to panic
Just what we all need

Stormy seas, times like these
Still they do just as they please
Just what we all need

Cheer Up Mr Morrissey – Have a Sausage Roll

#466 / 01:06:2021

Now there's a chappy we all know
Opinionated so and so
Miserable as heaven knows – so witty and so droll
This charmless man's a real pain
His big mouth, it strikes again
Cheer up Mr Morrissey – have a sausage roll

You might say that meat is murder
Don't you beef about my burger
Bacon tofu's more absurder – like vegan toad in the hole
November spawned a Monster Munch
Every day's like Sunday lunch
Cheer up Mr Morrissey – have a sausage roll

William it was really nothing
A hot pork roll with extra stuffing
Some girls are bigger than others
Especially if they're pasty lovers
My girlfriend was in a coma
Until she sniffed that pie's aroma
Heaven knows I'm miserable now
Sheila – Sheila – take a cow

Principles you may believe in
Don't you love a fascist vegan
All hail Ayatollah Stephen – he thinks he's in control
Some might say it's heresy
To criticize his deity
But cheer up Mr Misery – have a sausage roll

Oh what difference does it make?
Just pass me that T-bone steak
You're the one for me fatty
I don't really fancy that beetroot patty
Pretty girls – they make the gravy
Shakespeare's sizzlers – oh so flavoury
I've started something I just can't finish
A bit like watching Paddy McGuinness

This joke isn't funny anymore
But at least I tried
Cheer up Mr Morrissey …
The boy with the quorn in his side

Hopefully a Never-Ending Haiku

#467 / 02:06:2021

No-one died today
May tomorrow be the same
And the day after

Thirty Minutes – Not Much to Ask, Is It?

#468 / 03:06:2021

Thirty minutes extra on the school day
Not much to ask, is it?
It's one idea

So is having a smaller class size
Or cutting teachers' workload
Paper time, not children time obviously …

Or not teaching fronted bastard adverbials
Or letting teachers have the flexibility
To teach the things that really matter

Or providing funds for
Sport, music, drama, the arts …
It's time to learn to love school again

The school day doesn't need lengthening
Just needs brightening
Not much to ask, is it?

Inspired

#469 / 04:06:2021

I am reading a book
Written by my friend Michael
I've always loved his poems
But more-so now

Short lines
Of power and emotion
The fight for life
The fight for his life
In detail

Intimate, raw, honest
And funny

We have chatted since online
Mostly bad puns, jokes
And eternal football disappointment

I hope I made him smile
As much as he did me

Back to the book

My heart fills up
As I read
So do my eyes
But I am glad
That I am reading
These poems
It meant that he lived
To tell the tale

Not everyone did

A Poet, a Singer, an Artist and a Glam Rock Drummer

#470 / 05:06:2021

I used to watch *Top of the Pops*
Wait for Slade
And wish I was part of the band

Wanted to be a rock star
Couldn't play guitar
Or sing
Shouldn't have stopped me I know
But it did

Songs remained unsung
Potential hits unrecorded
But thanks to Roger McGough
And the Bard of Salford
Song words became poetry
So things went from bad to verse

Fast forward
Over forty years

Poetry returns to lyrics
For my friend Les to sing
While Martin designs logos and covers

There is a drummer too
The man all three of us watched on telly
Is our mate
And we are all in a band together

Strange how things turn out
But here we all are

Combined age of over
Two hundred and fifty

There may not be a *Top of the Pops*
But we do have an album
Out very soon
An actual vinyl album as well as the CD

Who'duv'thunk it bak then
When wee orl sang along but cudn't spel?

I'm Glad It Was With You

#471 / 06:06:2021

For Martyn Joseph

First live show since ... well
Forever
And the lights are down

We are far enough apart
To be safe
But close enough to be together

And it feels good
No
It feels great

No bookcases
No screens
No mute buttons

Hearing the hubbub of anticipation
Looking at the waiting guitars
Whose silent silver strings will soon sing gold

There will be applause
Connection and magic
The communion of artist and audience

And so much more
Heart and empathy
Wisdom, warmth and laughter

We sang along
Relishing the opportunity
Cherishing these moments

Sharing the intimacy
Celebrating the occasion
Yearning for more nights just like this

And Martyn, my friend
Oh my soul
I'm so, so glad it was with you

Carry on Crowing
#472 / 07:06:2021

Noisy crows today
Not so much a dawn chorus
More like drone caw-ers

Maybe raucous rooks
Who knows? Either way it is
Carrion squawking

Yes, they may be black
And yes, they may be birds, but
Still they cannot sing

Stumped

#473 / 08:06:2021

Historical tweets
Racist and sexist

From a teenage cricketer
Who should have known better

Historical comments
Racist and sexist

From a Prime Minister
Who should have known better

If one is wrong
So are both

If one is in
The other shouldn't be out

Lee Anderson and Brendan Clarke-Smith –
Thank You for Your Wisdom

#474 / 09:06:2021

(All the quotes in this poem are actual quotes from the Conservative politicians for Ashfield and Bassetlaw.)

There is something wrong
Really wrong
Rotten rancid wrong
When politicians talk about
"big mistakes"
"insults to intelligence"
Being "lectured on morality"
Or "a political movement whose core principles
aim to undermine our very way of life"

Strong words indeed
But bollocks

These are footballers
United against racism
Footballers standing up to hate
Footballers saying no to monkey noises
Footballers saying we believe in equality
And taking the knee is a simple visual symbol

What do you not understand?
Or
What do you not want to understand?

These are footballers
Not politicians in a powerful party
That has consistently made "big mistakes"
Consistently "lectured on morality"
Consistently "insulted our intelligence"
And are part of a "political movement whose core principles
aim to undermine our very way of life"

With every policy that affects the poor and disadvantaged
Every food bank opened
Every school meal withheld
Every nurse undervalued
Every hospital underfunded
Every lie told
And every corrupt favour accepted

"Sick and tired of being preached and spoken down to"?
Dead right
You bet we are

"Ridiculous empty gestures"?
Well at least you know exactly
What you are talking about there

Plus
National Empathy Day is tomorrow

National Empathy Day

#475 / 10:06:2021
(In seven rhyming haiku verses.)

I will empathise
With Tory politicians
By telling more lies

I won't take the knee
With all those other bigots
To show empathy

None of this is true
But you should always try to
See a point of view

It's empathy day
So look at situations
From another way

Don't leave out the 'a'
And 'h' for then it will be
One more empty day

If we need this day
If we have to spell it out
Things are not okay

What of tomorrow?
If we need reminding then
All this is hollow

Truth
A commodity not valued

Or
A commodity truly valued

As
Politicians seem to be economic with it

Rafa and Novak – We Salute You

#477 / 12:06:2021

I know
I'd promised to write a football poem
Every day
Already I've failed

Apparently Italy won
And played very well indeed
But I was elsewhere

Transfixed by tennis
Hypnotised by majesty
Mesmerised by drama
Hooked on brilliance

I could not tear myself away

Just when you thought it couldn't get better
It did
Just when you thought momentum had changed
It hadn't
Just when you thought the balance of power was shifting
It wasn't
Just when you thought history would repeat
It didn't

Gladiatorial at the very least
Face to face and toe to toe
Genius outdoes genius
Again and again and again
Superlatives run dry

Artistry and grit
Sweat and toil
Spectacle and spectacular
Magnificence personified

Four hours
Four hours
Not ninety minutes
Four hours
Of blockbuster sport
Box office entertainment
And the standards never faltered

This was the court of the red clay king
And the king was dethroned
Just
Only just
Small margins
Massive victory

When the gods played for us

When Everyone Prays for the Same Result

#478 / 13.06:2021
For Christian Eriksen

Football isn't usually a matter
Of life or death
But when it is
It is united

The Poetry Section at Waterstones

#479 / 14:06:2021

Whiling away an hour in a bookshop
Like a moth
I am drawn to poetry's flame

Not just to check if I am there
Although I always do
Even if it's just an anthology index

Children's section
Not a real section – *Fairy Tales and Gifts*
And I am invariably present

Being both egotistical and anonymous
I leave my book cover facing forward on the shelf
So the next customer sees me

Before Roald Dahl
Or Carol Ann Duffy, let's say
It makes no difference

Adult section, although copious
I am always absent
But this is no surprise

Looking first for favourites
McGough, Patten, Cooper Clarke
Ayres, Heaney and Billy Collins

I flick through pages of others
Those I'm told I should have read
Those I'm told I should be reading
Those I'm told are seminal or important

Vibrant new voices for the future
Important voices from the past

And invariably, I'm disappointed
Not because the words are not good
Just … just …

I'm yearning for something to reach out
Grab me by the heart
And say "live without me"

Something that says "buy me now"
A phrase, line, pun or joke
Wisdom I can't wait to read again

Words I want to savour
Words I can't wait to share with others
But I'm left … wanting

Wanting more
More than this
More than these

And also knowing
That for the same price
I'd probably get one-and-a-half Stephen Kings

Instead of a slim volume
With no real cover design
And a price that puts you off even taking a chance

Still, it is indeed an hour well spent
In good company, surrounded by pages
Just waiting to find their rightful reader

Even Vera Lynn Singing Wouldn't Help

#480 / 15:06:2021

Freedom Day it isn't
So here we are again

We know one day we'll meet
Don't know where
Don't know when

Neither does Boris

Everyone for Tennis?

#481 / 16:06:2021

Everyone for Wimbledon
Capacity crowd
Wembley Stadium
Half allowed

Looking for consistency
When socially distant
You are consistently
Inconsistent

So, We're All Agreed Then?

#482 / 17:06:2021

Well, it came to this?
Who would have thought it?
The country united
So, we're all agreed then

All as one
Unanimously
We are all in total agreement
With our Prime Minister

You have your Churchill moment
You have said something
No-one could possibly disagree with
Or take exception to

Unless you are, of course
Mr Hancock
Who is indeed
"Totally ****ing hopeless"

Something we all knew
And have done
For a very long time
Which begs the question ...

If that is the case
And you knew
Why didn't you do something?
Why is he still in his job?

Or is it just good
To have someone
More hopeless than yourself
To distract us all?

When Old Rivalries Renew

#483 / 18:06:2021

It's the battle of old enemies
And Euro bragging rights
Much more than just three points
And the perfect Friday night
It's the winning, it's the winning
And it doesn't matter how
Any lucky rebound counts
It's the here and it's the now
No-one wants to lose
A last gasp draw may do
In the battle of the Euros
When old rivalries renew

Form goes out the window
It's the passion on the day
The team that wants it most
Not the systems that we play
The feuding and the histories
The bitter memories
Decisions made against us
By dodgy referees
The blood and guts and bravery
The will to get us through
In the battle of the Euros
When old rivalries renew

The times we smashed it totally
The taste of victories
The times when losing we lost face
To colleagues, friends and families
Desperate to come out top
Desperate to score

Losing's not an option
We might just take a draw
And if the ball ends in the net
We really don't care who
Is the hero on the day
When old rivalries renew

The hopes we have at kick off
Reality arrives
The bitten fingernails
This rollercoaster ride
The tension, nerves, excitement
This time we'll get it right
The feeling in our water
That this time we just might
Raise our game that extra notch
So we can turn the screw
And get one over on them
When old rivalries renew

And at the end of the day
It's more than just a game
Whatever the result
Things never stay the same
We may feel over the moon
Cheer and celebrate
Or sick as dogs and parrots
As we commiserate
And there's always next time
The heart remains so true
In the duel of the year
When old rivalries renew

Great Expectations

Underperformed
Overawed
Didn't lose
At least it's a draw

Back down to earth
Usual state
Expectations
Always grate

Always a Book

#485 / 20:06:2021

In latter years
It was always a book
I can't remember what
It was when I was younger
But in the latter years
It was always a book
Invariably hardback
Seemed classier, appropriate
Often football related
Church-based or biography
Sometimes just a good story
That I know you'd read quickly

Today, I think of all the books
I haven't bought with you in mind
Although you are always in mind
Always close by, a constant barometer
I wonder what you would make of today
The modern world and its changes
Our achievements and disappointments
All the things I never got to tell you
All the football we never watched
You remembered sixty-six, never yet repeated
So today, I will reach to my bookshelf
Take down a book and open a page
You never raised an alcoholic toast
But today I raise these words to you

There was always a book with dad
And not just on Father's Day

Fifty-Six Years On

At primary school
We talked of football, football, football
Music and what we watched on the telly

Now
We still talk of football, football, football
Music, what we watched on the telly

But also
Hip replacements
Keyhole knee surgery
Heart problems and cancer
Care homes and funerals
Captaining the bowls club

And
Missed sixtieth birthday parties

When someone who has
Failed and wasted public funds
Is even thought of

We have rolled over
And you prepare to rub our
Noses in the dirt

Apparently, we should have been back to normal by now
(Whatever that may be) – but we're not

However, variant numbers on the rise and everyone thinks
It'll be okay because we have a vaccine – but it's not

And in the midst of all this confusion
Inconsistencies arise with alarming consistency
As the government seems to tie itself and then us – into knots

Every Day is Thank a Teacher Day

#489 / 24:06:2021
For National Thank a Teacher Day

You want me to call you "Joan"
But I can't
Not really
Always Mrs Burton

Fifty years ago
(Yes, I know …)
You stood at the front of our class
Day by day
And taught us all the things
We now take for granted

We cannot remember the learning
You channelled that osmosis
On a daily basis
And all I remember
Is that it was a good time
A great time

A time of stories and writing
A time of painting and drawing
Art, craft, playing
And the collaboration of learning

Sitting by the window with Wiggy
Heatlumps, Ammo and Lewo
Always close by
A time we all enjoyed

We must have done grammar
But not like today
Thank goodness

And here we are
Fifty years later
(Yes, I know ...)
All still here
And you, still commenting on my poems
Not marking them
But telling me it's the best homework
I've ever done
And me, still relishing those comments
Loving the fact that you love these poems

Even though I can call you "Joan"
I still think Mrs Burton
I still thank Mrs Burton
Thank you

Joan

No Weddings, More Funerals

#490 / 25:06:2021

Not a good title for a comedy film
But we are getting to that stage
That uncertain age
Everyday aches and pains
Conditions our grandparents complained of
Health we once took for granted
Where an unexpected telephone call
Or email out of the blue
Is often news we rather we didn't have to hear
Failing health, sudden illnesses
Hospital visits and operations
Cancer conversations seem regular these days
Closer to the end than the beginning
Not every story has a happy ending
That uncertain age

Clear as Mud

#491 / 25:06:2021

You can watch the fastest racing cars
But not those who play guitars

Watch and cheer a winning goal
But you can't rock and you can't roll

See the horses, race and bet
Theatres ain't seen nothing yet

It's everyone for tennis
But gigs ... who knows when is

The time for all these rules to change
Treat everybody just the same

Instead, as usual, we discover
One rule for some, one rule for others

At No Point Will This Poem Descend into Cheap Puns Regarding the Unfortunate Nature of His Surname And the Current Situation He Finds Himself In Which is Obviously a Private Matter

#492 / 26:06:2021

If he can do it, nothing to it – a snog and then a grope
The man who was hopeless is giving all men hope
Now we know why track and trace didn't have a clue
When Mrs H couldn't find a track and trace on you

Hands, face, space – just what could it mean?
Your hands – her face – no space in between
Two metres apart – not your way of life
Until you get home – much more with your wife

Stay home – save lives – advice that you have known
Not sure that's the case when you go home
You might meet matrimonial resistance
You're going to find the real meaning of social distance

Lies and deception – nothing really sinister
Just in training to be the next Prime Minister
Horror! Surprise! Revulsion! Shock!
The two go together – Matt and Cock

I know the title said I wouldn't sink as low as that
But I was telling lies – just like Matt
Cheap and puerile, perhaps I'd better stop
The two go together – Matt and Cock

That's below the belt – a real cheap shot
Just like Matt – just like his …

A Message on Behalf of the Prime Minister

#493 / 27:06:2021

I just want you to know
That I always backed him
His job was always safe
I would not have sacked him

You may ask me why
Just how can that be
Well, it's good to have someone
Who's a bigger pratt than me

Papers at a Bus Stop in a Random Street in Kent

#494 / 28.06:2021

We all believe in freedom – and freedom of speech
Freedom of information – but security's been breached
Just how could it happen? What was the intent
With papers at a bus stop in a random street in Kent?

Soggy, strewn and sensitive – and not for prying eyes
The governmental density that nothing can disguise
Secrecy and service – just not evident
With papers at a bus stop in a random street in Kent

What's the plan? Afghanistan? Maybe the Black Sea
The rushing of the Russians against our M.O.D.
Not much of a plan that they try to implement
With papers at a bus stop in a random street in Kent

Possible manoeuvres for H.M.S. Defender
No papers marked with "please return to sender"
But the BBC and licence fee – money that's well spent
For papers at a bus stop in a random street in Kent

So who lives in Kent? Who travels on a bus?
Shouldn't be that hard to find – who caused all the fuss
So what are the excuses that they're trying to invent
For the papers at a bus stop in a random street in Kent

But procedures are in place – hoping to ensure
That this sort of accident won't happen any more
Going to stop the problem – this is what they meant
They're going to take away all the bus stops there in Kent

Dear Gareth ... Dear England

#495 / 29:06:2021

You have a unique opportunity
You carry the hopes and dreams of a nation

May they lift you and give you feet of fire
May they free you to play with risk and reward
May they inspire you to greater things
And may the spirit inside burn brighter, stronger, longer

Do not be afraid of history
Do not be weighed down by doubt
Do not be shackled by negativity
Do not be held back for fear of falling

In any match
One team must lose
And one team must win
That is how it always is
But that is what excites us
Jeopardy and opportunity – hand in hand
Success and failure – both within our grasp

Already this will be a lifelong memory
Already this will be a snapshot
A pivotal moment that we experience together

But you have the chance to make it special
Really special
You have the chance to be immortal
You have the chance to be heroes
The chance to be legends

You are doing what we could only dream of
What most of us have dreamed ot
So make those dreams come true
And win

Win for us
Win for England

Or

Lose – but if that is the way it must be
Then lose by being brave
Run till you can run no more
Put your bodies on that line
Dig deep
Then deeper still
Do not leave that field of dreams
With anything left to give
With anything you should have done

Just make us proud
Then make us prouder still

Let the lions roar
Until they can roar no more

Do this and we shall remember this moment forever

Dear Gareth – dear England
History awaits

Thank You

#496 / 30:06:2021

Thank you Gareth and Raheem
Thank you Harry, thank you team

Ghosts are vanquished, curses lifted
Hoodoo banished, demons dealt with

A nation breathes, a nation sighs
Fires kindle, hopes arise

Celebration and relief
Realisation and belief

Thank you England, thank you team
Dare we hope, dare we dream …

Not Clever, Not Witty, Just Stupid

#497 / 01:07:2021

Protestors protesting
About the freedom to believe
What they think is the truth
Harass a man
Who has the freedom to believe
What he thinks is the truth

Louder Than You

#498 / 02:07:2021

Well, you shout about the empire
You shout about the flag
You shout for Queen and country
And the greatness we once had
You shout about our history
But not about today
Yes, you who shout the loudest
Have nothing much to say

You shout about the football
About the price of beer
You shout about the refugees
Escaping over here
You're full of smoke and mirrors
It's hot air and it's gas
Cos you who shout the loudest
Are talking through your ass

Silence may be golden
But it's time now to be loud
Time to raise our voices
And shout above the crowd
For those who raise their voices
Are those who dare to doubt
All you who shout the loudest
With the least to shout about

We're going to shout it loud and proud
Together, trusted, true
Shout it louder till we are
Louder than you

Shout out every single truth
Every single word
Carry on our shouting
Till our voices can be heard
From the rising of the sun
To the shining of the moon
We'll shout while we are dancing
To a different freedom tune

We're going to shout for justice
We're going to shout for peace
Equality not poverty
Resolution and release
Shout that lives all matter
Until our throats are raw
And when you think we're beaten ...
Then we'll shout a little more!

And

Drown out your distraction
Drown out all your lies
Drown your pointless waffle
And needless compromise
Drown out your intolerance
These fires that you stoke
Drown your bigotry with love
And drown your hate with hope

We're going to shout it loud and proud
Shout it once again
Just remember this
Hate won't win

Heads We Win, Tails You Lose
#499 / 03:07:2021

Wimbledon and Wembley, a myriad smiling faces
Parents who cannot attend their children's sports day races

Two sides of the coin – one a win and one a loss
I suppose it all depends on just who gives a toss

Poem Five Hundred

04:07:2021

Poem five hundred – in less than two years
Daily undertaking, creative exercise

Writing routinely – but not routinely writing
A habit formed I don't want to break

Surprising myself – loving the challenge
Some things I knew, something that's new

All these poems – I would never have written
All these words, asleep, undisturbed

Each day I wake – shake them all up
Each day they fall, find their own shape

Each poem a journey – new and exciting
Less than two years, five hundred poems

What Started as a Whisper ...

#501 / 05:07:2021

There's a humming in the streets
A buzzing in the air
Three words of a song
Seem to echo everywhere

Belief is getting stronger
With every goal we score
What started as a whisper
Has now become a roar

Caution, trepidation
Weighed down by the past
And a nation's desperation
To make this moment last

All the pain and all the hurt
We've all been there before
But what started as a whisper
Has now become a roar

Exceeding expectation
Unbeaten in our task
A time for celebration
The prize within our grasp

Games completed, undefeated
Now it's time to soar
What started as a whisper
Has now become a roar

This chapter in the story
Now becoming real
This dream of hope and glory
Something new that we all feel

We never dared to dream
What the future had in store
What started as a whisper
Has now become a roar

Nearly there, don't falter now
One match at a time
Nothing much to alter now
Things are going fine

Opportunity is knocking
Unlocking every door
What started as a whisper
Has now become a roar

The who and what and why and how
Just keep Raheem and Harry on
We don't think it's over now
Just want it all to carry on

Let this now be the time
When football's home once more
What started as a whisper
Has now become a roar

today's poem is a freedom poem there are no
restrictions on genre style or rhythm and no
guidelines regarding rhymes on lines internal
or otherwise they are there but it is up to you
to recognise them that is your own personal
choice this poem has words you may choose to
read or completely ignore again that is totally
your own choice and up to your own personal
interpretation should you want to break these
words up into verses with spaces in between
well that is up to you as everything is here and
you can look at all the information and rewrite
the poem accordingly true there is no structure
and the lack of punctuation may confuse the fact
that the words are somewhat crowded together
perhaps appearing a little muddled but isn't that
what you wanted some creative freedom and room
to manoeuvre with no-one telling you how it all
should be so yes this is a normal poem but it is up
to you how to interpret it because that is your own
personal responsibility plus the fact because you
have read a poem on the internet you are suddenly
an expert and know all about poetry so go ahead
be free be free be free be free be free be free be

Sometimes

#503 / 07:07:2021

Sometimes
It's just the act
Of picking up a pen
And putting pen to paper
That makes the magic happen

Three Lines on Those Shirts

#504 / 08:07:2021

One last match, a final step
One more hurdle, one more time
Finally, finally, finally reached that finishing line

Why Wouldn't You?
Just to Be on the Safe Side and Think of Others

#505 / 08:07:2021

My answer to the question
Should you choose to ask
Even after "Freedom Day"
I'll choose to wear my mask

Fever Pitch

#506 / 09:07:2021

As football fever
Grips the nation
Let us hope and pray
That it is indeed football
And not the fever
That grips the nation

Nothing to Do With Football

#507 / 10:07:2021

We have been living
With the Johnson Variant
For far too long now
All this Brexit talk
And now he just wants England
To win the Euros

Will of the Nation

#508 / 11:07:2021

I will stand – side by side
Wave the flag, salute the shirt
Celebrate this magic
For all the years of so-called hurt

Enjoy all the euphoria
Give my full support
But I will not boo an anthem
In the name of sport

I will not sneer at those who kneel
Will not whistle, will not jeer
Instead, I'll raise my voice and sing
When my chosen team appear

I will dream of dreams victorious
And all England expects
Whatever happens on the night
Respect – respect – respect

At Last

#509 / 11:07:2021

So here we are
Not many of us have been here before
On the cusp of history
We may have dreamed about this moment
And thought it the impossible
But here we are
Here we all are
United behind a team
Who are united behind their leader
In days when leaders
Have shown themselves to be
Untrustworthy, fickle and shallow
It is good to see a man
Address the nation with respect
Address the nation with honesty
A man not afraid to make his choices
A man with a plan that he will follow through
A man with integrity and dignity
It may be only football
But feels like so much more
The feel-good factor that feels so good
And whatever the score
You have already won our hearts
Already run that extra mile
And should we fall at that final hurdle
You will still be heroes
The ones who restored confidence and belief
And for that
We salute you, Gareth Southgate
We salute you, England

The Morning After the Night Before

#510 / 12:07:2021

Once more the same old feelings
So here we are again
Almost there, but not quite right
Once again – the nearly men

A thumping start to raise the heart
A goal that raised the bar
Despite the hope – we couldn't cope
So close and yet so far

The final hurdle just too high
We've all been here before
We couldn't do the Italian job
And blow the bloody door

Out thought, out fought, just overwrought
Close but no cigar
The mentality of penalties
So close and yet so far

Foundations, firm and fearless
Lots to be proud about
Reasons to be cheerful
More than usual to shout about

Not there yet – so just re-set
And build from where we are
Learn the lessons from the loss
So close and yet so far

No shame and no disgrace
Not much more we could have done
Perhaps a touch more bravery
And who knows what we could have won

But you have won again the hearts
Let's wish upon this star
And hope it keeps on rising
So close and yet so far

Opposition

#511 / 13:07:2021

The team that we support at home
Have now made the decision
To stand up against all that is wrong
We support their opposition

The team that we all love the most
Have stated their position
To stand together against hate
We support their opposition

Dignity, morality
These men now on a mission
More than just a football team
We support the opposition

Small Change

#512 / 14:07:2021

If you begin with *hate*
And that is all you *have*
Stuck inside that darkened *cave*
You don't even really *care*
So to get right to the very *core*
Of the problem and try to *cope*
Until we bring about *hope*
Could be a journey that's long
But this is the bottom line
We can get from hate to hope
But it might be one letter at a time

Freedom?

#513 / 15:07:2021

As the date draws ever closer
The question is not whether
I will wear my mask
But more
Will I still write a poem every day?

I suspect the answer to both
Will probably be the same

Recipe for Disaster

#514 / 16:07:2021

"The ketchup of the catch up
The yeast that lifts, the magic sauce"
Verbal garnish that's the varnish
To distract from no main course

A mayonnaise to ease malaise
Guacamole to level-up wholly
Salad cream of egalitarian dream
Crunchy coleslaw – less is more

The mustard for the flustered
Horseradish of the mad and faddish
The gravy of gravitas – maybe
The barbecue glaze of better days

The relish of embellishment
A pickle for the fickle
The salt and pepper of the never-never
Chunky chutney for the gluttony

Madly mixed-up metaphors
Keep everybody guessing
Condiments of condescension
All just empty dressing

Common Nonsense

#515 / 17:07:2021

Follow the science
Follow the maths
Look at the facts
The spikes and the graphs
Statistics don't lie
So please may I ask
Is this the right time
To dispense with the masks?

Too Hot for a Hike

#516 / 18:07:2021

Today's poem may be late
I've gone for a walk before it's too hot

A Pilot With No Navigation System

#517 / 18:07:2021

The Prime Minister
Says he is using
The pilot scheme

He is

The Pontius Pilate Scheme
Washing his hands of all responsibility

And has been doing so
For far too long

Freedom Day Sonnet

#518 / 19:07:2021

Cooped up for too long, Freedom Day at last
No longer confined, no more concerns
Cast away caution and chuck all your masks
Good riddance, goodbye, normal life returns

Farewell restrictions, go put them behind
Open your arms to the shops and the bars
Personal freedom for all and you'll find
Chaos will reign in this country of ours

No matter what's wrong, no matter what's right
There is one thing that you must understand
I'll do what I want and go where I like
Rampant and raging, I'll course through this land

On the same page as Covid deniers
Freedom is mine – says Coronavirus

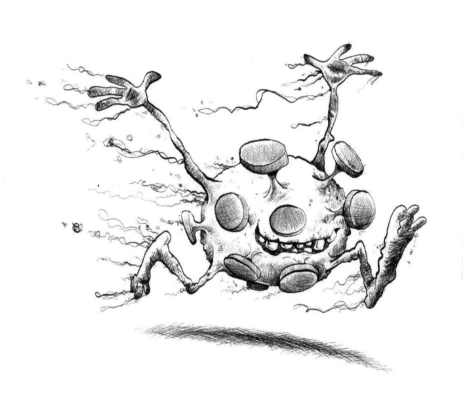

I can only dedicate this book to all you wonderful online friends who have commented, liked and shared these poems with me on a daily basis. Without you …

"Our national treasure." *Judy Camp*

"It has been a great commentary of these unusual and frightening times. Just wish the Prime Minister had been reading with us. Keep them coming please." *Jamie Bannister*

"Absolute genius." *Julie Slater*

"Thoughtful and intelligent – pity our government isn't too!" *Jen Tyler Stevens*

"Spot on." *John Wat Tyler Parton*

"Over the many months your poems have displayed more leadership and sane advice than 60-plus million have received from the government. Thank you." *Richard Cox*

"Thanks for keeping so many of us going." *Sue Wilson*

"You are an inspiration." *Sally Thompson*

"I've looked forward to reading your poems every morning." *Nomis Simon Baurley*

"Perfectly put." *Janice Johnson*

"Lovely ridicule." *Andy Camp*

"Perfect analysis … Your poems have helped us all so much. You have so often, and so skilfully, put my own thoughts into beautiful / angry / amusing / heart-breaking verse. I am still reading your books on a 12-months-on basis and very often the words are just as relevant. Thank you – you have been a light in the darkness." *Janet New*

"Greatly blessed by your efforts. Nailed it again!" *Steve Thorpe*

"Impressively cutting." *Janet Cuthbert*

"Your skill with words is amazing and your discipline is second to none. I'm so proud of you." *Joan Burton*

"Fantastic – spot on." *Mark Cawdery*

"So true." *Louise Dunsire*

"Thanks for doing this Paul – we need it." *Catherine Obbard*

"Such a huge achievement. We are all so grateful to have your poems every day. They're so varied and have kept us laughing, crying and kept us going. Thank you so much." *Claire Bartrip*

"Fantastic stuff." *Garry Clarkson*

"Great work." *Keith Baxter*

"Says it like it is." *Moira Andrew*

"Thank you for your words of wisdom. Some have made me laugh out loud, others have made me rage with you, and one or two have made me cry." *Jane Box*

"I love the way you speak for all of us – but so much better than we could." *Shirley Smith*

"Fabulous – very proud of you." *Kim Hopper*

"Brilliant … again." *Mark Heybourne*

"Excellent – hits the spot." *Deirdre Speed*

"Something to look forward to on a daily basis." *Harvinder Evans*

"Made my day!" *Katie Holdstock*

"Your daily poems brighten my day." *Bev Rodham*

"Amen!" *Neil Mitchell*

Thanks a million to you all …
and everyone else who has commented on a regular basis.
You are my audience and your comments are my virtual applause.

Fighting Talk – Vol. 1

Illustrated by Chris Riddell OBE

Composed throughout the initial phase of the UK's coronavirus lockdown, these poems cover the period of 23rd March to 3rd July 2020.

"Manages to season his cogent observations of COVID-19 with a dash of humour that makes you want to dip in again and again." *Valerie Bloom MBE*

"Witty and wise, astute and acerbic." *Tony Walsh*

"He's never going to let a worldwide pandemic curb his creativity. COVID-19 will give up before he does." *Henry Normal*

Can of Worms – Vol. 2

Illustrated by Martin Chatterton

These poems document the period of July to mid-October 2020 – from the pubs re-opening through to the introduction of the 'Three-Tier System'.

"These trying times need poets to help us find a compass. This book is a must." *Michael Rosen*

"Gives voice to all the things that scare us and all the things that lift us, and everything in between." *Rev. Kate Bottley*

"A sublime collection of instinctive and honest poems." *Badly Drawn Boy*

Pig's Ear, Dog's Dinner – Vol. 3

Illustrated by Korky Paul

Covers the period from the introduction of the 'Thre Tier System' (and our subsequent bonus fourth tier! through to the anniversary of the first lockdown.

"In these strange times, every day should have a P Cookson moment." *Simon Mayo*

"If journalism is the first draft of history, then here is th second: life shaped, structured, described, annotated *Ian McMillan*

"A must-read memento of these challenging times. Brilliant." *Paul Ross*

Available in paperback and eBook
flapjackpress.co.uk